All About Magnifying Glasses

by Melvin Berger
illustrated by Elroy Freem

SCHOLASTIC INC.
New York Toronto London Auckland Sydney

For Max and Jake
—M.B.

With thanks to Dr. Anthony Ting, Stanford University,
for his assistance in preparing this book.

ISBN 0-590-45510-9

Copyright © 1993 by the Melvin H. and Gilda Berger Trust.
All rights reserved. Published by Scholastic Inc.

12 11 10 9 8 7 6 5 4 3 2 1   3 4 5 6 7 8/9
Printed in the U.S.A.   08
First Scholastic printing, February 1993

Magnifying glasses are amazing tools.
They can help you in many ways.
They make small things look bigger
than they really are.
They sometimes let you see things that you
can't see with your eyes alone.

DO IT YOURSELF

Magnify Letters

Look at the words in this book.
Notice the size of the letters.

Now find the magnifying glass
at the end of this book.
Take it out carefully.

Hold the magnifying glass over this page.
Look at the same words through the glass.
What do you see?

The letters seem to be bigger.
Of course, the letters do not change their size.
They only look bigger through
the magnifying glass.

How do you see the letters without
a magnifying glass?

Light is like a ball.
Drop it and it bounces back.

Light comes from the sun or a light bulb.
The rays of light strike the page.
The light bounces back.
It enters your eyes.
And you are able to see the letters.

How does a magnifying glass make letters
look bigger?

The magnifying glass is a lens.
A lens is a curved piece of glass or plastic
that is thicker in the middle.
It is called a convex lens.

Light passes through the convex lens.
The lens bends the light.
The light spreads apart.
The spread out light makes the letters look bigger.

Think of a hose that people use to water a lawn.
A ray of light is like the water flowing
through the hose.

Now think of a sprinkler at the end of the hose.
The sprinkler spreads out the stream of water.
The spray is like light after it passes through
the magnifying glass.

DO IT YOURSELF

Magnify Everyday Objects

Collect:

- a newspaper photo.
- a few grains of salt.
- a few grains of pepper.
- a dollar bill.
- a shiny new dime.

First look at each object without the magnifying glass.
Then look at them through the magnifying glass.
With the magnifying glass, you'll see some
amazing things.

The newspaper photo is made up of tiny dots.
The grains of salt have smooth sides.
The pepper edges are rough and pointy.
The dollar bill has colored threads in the paper.
The dime has initials just under the head.

What other things do you notice?

You know that your magnifying glass is
a convex lens.
But did you know that you have other
convex lenses at home?
A round jar with liquid inside works
like a convex lens.

DO IT YOURSELF

Find Convex Lenses Around the House

Find a round glass jar of olives, beans,
or cherries.
Look through the glass.
Notice the size of the objects inside.
See how big they look.

Now take out a few olives, beans, or cherries.
See how small they really are.

The objects inside the jar look bigger because
the jar is like a convex lens.
Outside the jar, the objects are their true size.

DO IT YOURSELF

Make a Convex Lens

Get a round drinking glass made of clear glass.
Fill it with water.

Put the glass on a table.
Hold a book behind the glass.

Look at the letters through the glass.
What do you see?

The letters look much larger.
The round glass of water is like a convex lens.

Poke your finger into the glass of water.
Look through the side of the glass at your finger.
The part of your finger in the water looks big and fat.

A round glass jar of water works like a convex lens.
So does a single drop of water.

DO IT YOURSELF

Form a Drop-of-Water Lens

Get a small paper clip.
Bend one end into a tiny loop.
You may need an adult to help you.
The loop should be as small and tight as possible.

Dip the loop into a glass of water.
A drop of water will form inside the loop.

The drop of water has the shape of a ball.
It is curved like a convex lens.
You can use the waterdrop as a magnifying glass.

Hold the drop of water over a newspaper.
Look at a single letter through the water lens.
Does it seem bigger than when you look
with your eyes alone?

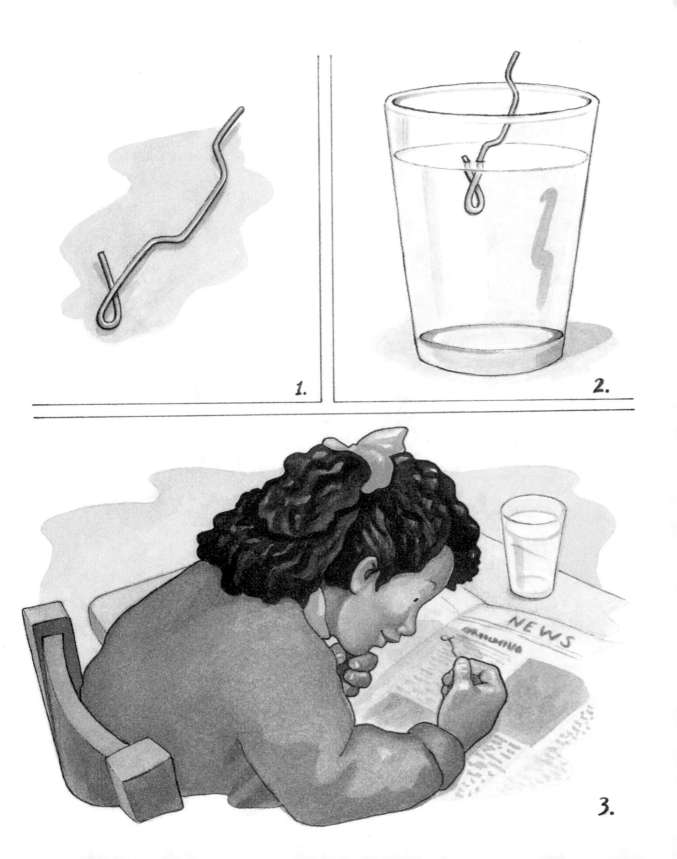

1.

2.

3.

Now get a small piece of clear plastic wrap.
Spread it out on the newspaper.
Dip your finger in a glass of water.
Let just one drop of water fall on to the plastic.

Look through the drop of water.
See how big it makes the letters.
The drop of water has become a convex lens.

Using two hands, gently lift the plastic
just above the newspaper.
Now everything looks even bigger.

A round jar can become a convex lens.
So can a drop of water.
But the most handy convex lens is your
magnifying glass.
It can help you find out more about yourself.

DO IT YOURSELF

Magnify Your Skin

Study the back of your hand through
the magnifying glass.
Do you see:

- little, fuzzy hairs?
- the lines over your knuckles?
- any freckles?

Now turn your hand over.
Place your palm under a strong light.
Look at it through the magnifying glass.
What do you see?

- A few thick lines?
- Lots of small lines?
- Many tiny holes?

The holes are pores.
Pores are openings in the skin.
Sweat comes out through the pores.

There is a lot to see on the back and palm of your hand.
But looking at fingerprints can be even more fun.

DO IT YOURSELF

Take Your Fingerprint

Find an ink pad, a sheet of clean paper,
and a paper towel.
Press the tip of one finger on the ink pad.
Then carefully press that fingertip on the paper.
Clean your inky finger with the paper towel.

Look through the magnifying glass
at your fingerprint.
Which fingerprint pattern do you have?

Is it a loop?
  The lines come in from one side and loop around.

Is it an arch?
  The lines go across, but rise in the middle.

Is it a circle?
  The lines circle around the center.

A magnifying glass lets you see
your fingerprint pattern.
You can also use the lens to see patterns in cloth.

Cloth is made of long, thin threads.
The threads sometimes form a crisscross pattern.
Crisscross means the cloth is woven.
Woven cloth feels smooth.

Other cloths have threads that loop around each other.
Looping stitches form knitted cloth.
Knitted cloth feels bumpy.

DO IT YOURSELF

Check Out Your Clothing

Look through the magnifying glass
at the clothes you are wearing.

Do the threads crisscross?
Is the cloth smooth?
That cloth is woven.

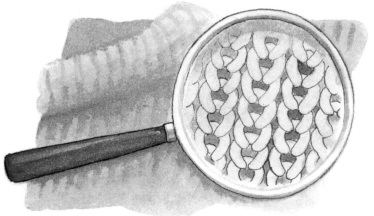

Can you see looping stitches?
Does the cloth feel rough and bumpy?
That cloth is knitted.

Suppose you get a stain on a piece of clothing?
Washing with detergent removes the stain.
Do you know why?

DO IT YOURSELF

Detergent to the Rescue

Collect:

- a rag of woven cloth.
- a drop of ketchup.
- some liquid detergent.
- a spoon.
- your magnifying glass.

Spread the cloth on a kitchen counter.
Make a small ketchup stain on the cloth.
Dip the handle of the spoon into the detergent.
Drop a bit of detergent on top of the ketchup stain.

Look at the stain through your magnifying glass.
Do you see the detergent soaking into the ketchup?
The detergent helps to pull the ketchup off the cloth.

A magnifying glass makes small things bigger.
But it also lets you turn things upside down!

DO IT YOURSELF

Make a Magnifying Glass Picture

Get a piece of clean white paper and
your magnifying glass.
Stand with your back to a sunny window.
(It helps if the shades or curtains are pulled
on other windows in the room.)

Hold the paper in front of you.
Move it to a side so you don't block the sunlight.

Put your magnifying glass between the paper
and the window.
Move the magnifying glass back and forth
between the window and the paper.
Move it until you see a clear picture on the paper.

The picture is the view from the window.
But something is funny.
The picture is upside down!

Suppose you see a man in front of the window.
It looks like he's standing on his head.

Here's why.
The light bouncing off his shoes passes up
through the magnifying glass.
It becomes the top of the picture.

The light bouncing off his hat passes down
through the magnifying glass.
It becomes the bottom of the picture.
That makes the man look upside down.

Go to the other windows.
Make other funny upside down pictures.

Use your magnifying glass here, there, everywhere.
Amaze yourself.
Amaze your friends!